The Volcanic Eruption of Santorini, 1650 BCE

Jim Whiting

P.O. Box 196
Hockessin, Delaware 19707
Visit us on the web: www.mitchelllane.com
Comments? email us:
mitchelllane@mitchelllane.com

Mitchell Lane PUBLISHERS

Copyright © 2007 by Mitchell Lane Publishers. All rights reserved. No part of this book may be reproduced without written permission from the publisher. Printed and bound in the United States of America.

Printing   1   2   3   4   5   6   7   8   9

A Robbie Reader/Natural Disasters

The Ancient Mystery of Easter Island
The Bermuda Triangle
Bubonic Plague
Earthquake in Loma Prieta, California, 1989
The Fury of Hurricane Andrew, 1992
Hurricane Katrina, 2005
The Lost Continent of Atlantis
Mt. Vesuvius and the Destruction of Pompeii, A.D. 79
Mudslide in La Conchita, California, 2005
Tsunami Disaster in Indonesia, 2004
Where Did All the Dinosaurs Go?
Tornado Outbreak 1985
The Volcanic Eruption of Santorini, 1650 BCE

Library of Congress Cataloging-in-Publication Data
Whiting, Jim, 1943-
  The volcanic eruption of Santorini, 1650 BCE / by Jim Whiting.
    p. cm. — (A Robbie Reader. Natural disasters)
  Includes bibliographical references and index.
  ISBN 978-1-58415-568-3 (library bound)
  1. Santorini Volcano (Greece)—History. 2. Santorini Volcano (Greece)—Eruptions. 3. Geology—Greece—Thera Island Region. 4. Volcanism—Greece—Thera Island Region. I. Title.
  QE523.S27W55 2008
  949.5'85—dc22

                                                                                                2007000816

ABOUT THE AUTHOR: Jim Whiting has been a remarkably versatile and accomplished journalist, writer, editor, and photographer for more than 30 years. He has made numerous trips to Greece, including three visits to Santorini. A voracious reader since early childhood, Mr. Whiting has written and edited more than 250 nonfiction children's books on a wide range of topics. He lives in Washington state with his wife and two teenage sons.

PHOTO CREDITS: pp. 4, 8, 11, 12—USGS; p. 14—University of Rhode Island; pp. 16, 17, 22, 24, 25, 26—Jim Whiting; p. 18—David Hardy/Photo Researchers; p. 20—Ivan Kashinsky; p. 21—Jonathan Scott; p. 27—Jaime Kondreck

PUBLISHER'S NOTE: The following story has been thoroughly researched and to the best of our knowledge represents a true story. While every possible effort has been made to ensure accuracy, the publisher will not assume liability for damages caused by inaccuracies in the data, and makes no warranty on the accuracy of the information contained herein.

To reflect current usage, we have chosen to use the secular era designations BCE ("before the common era") and CE ("of the common era") instead of the traditional designations BC ("before Christ") and AD (*anno Domini*, "in the year of the Lord").

                                                                                                              PLB

TABLE OF CONTENTS

Words in **bold** type can be found in the glossary.

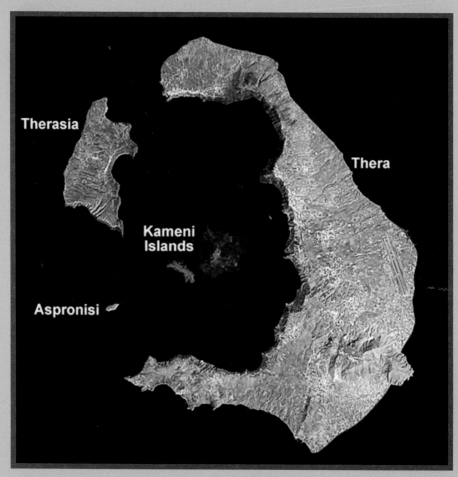

Modern-day Santorini as seen from space. The island was formed by
a volcano. More than 3,600 years ago, a huge eruption split the
island into three parts: Thera, Therasia, and Aspronisi. Later, smaller
eruptions made the Kameni Islands, including Nea Kameni (center)
and Palea Kameni (green, center).

Living the Good Life

Thousands of years ago, the citizens of Akrotiri (ak-roh-TEER-ee) were living very well. Their town was on the island of Calliste, between Greece and Crete in the Aegean (uh-JEE-un) Sea. On a modern-day map, Calliste is called Santorini (san-tuh-REE-nee).

Crete was also quite **civilized**, and the two islands traded goods. Sailors would leave Calliste in the morning and arrive at Crete before dark. They would spend a few days exchanging their products and seeing the sights. Then they would sail home.

The climate in the Aegean was ideal. The sun shone regularly during most of the year, and people enjoyed being outdoors.

Ancient murals show how people lived on Calliste. From the murals, we know that fish were important to the people of Calliste.

The people on Calliste also enjoyed their large homes. Some houses had two, three, or even four stories. A few had as many as thirty rooms. Homeowners could afford to have artists paint murals on their walls. Many of these murals have survived through the centuries. They showed workers such as fishermen. They also showed well-dressed people who ate good food and liked animals. Some families even had monkeys for pets.

In most other parts of the world, people rarely bathed. Some never did. The people of Akrotiri, though, kept themselves clean. They could take hot baths often.

Their town was also very clean. In other places, people simply emptied **sewage** onto the streets. The filth caused terrible odors and helped spread disease. In Akrotiri, flush toilets emptied into an underground sewage system.

It's no wonder that the inhabitants called their island Calliste. The word means "most beautiful." They had enjoyed their way of life for hundreds of years. They didn't know they were living on a time bomb.

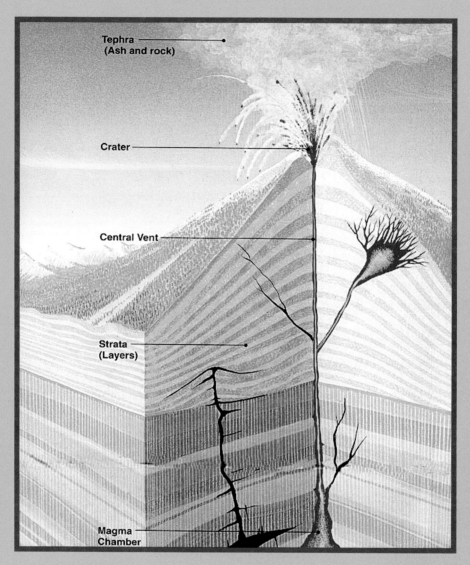

Tephra (Ash and rock)

Crater

Central Vent

Strata (Layers)

Magma Chamber

A volcano forms when hot magma pushes up through the earth's surface. Lava and tephra (ash and rock) spew from the crater. As the lava flows down the side of the mountain and cools, it adds another layer to the volcano.

Explosive Islands

The island of Calliste was actually a **volcano** that had slowly built up from the bottom of the ocean.

The ground we walk on appears solid, but a few thousand feet under the surface, it isn't. There, the earth is very hot. The surface floats on a layer of hot gases and melted rock called **magma** (MAG-mah). Magma and the hot gases produce a lot of pressure. When the pressure gets too great, the magma and gases erupt through cracks or weak spots in the ground.

When the magma meets air or cold water, it is known as **lava** (LAH-vah). As the lava cools, it forms a little hill. Over many years, the hill gets higher and higher. It can reach thousands of feet above the ground or above the bed of the sea.

Many islands have been formed by volcanoes, including the Hawaiian Islands. The first of these volcanic islands rose above the surface of the ocean a little over 5 million years ago. Since then, several more have emerged.

Kilauea (kee-lao-WAY-uh) on the Big Island of Hawaii is the world's largest currently active volcano. It has been erupting almost constantly since 1983. Lava that flows from Kilauea can destroy property. Volcanoes on the other islands are **dormant**. That means they are "sleeping," or not erupting. Scientists believe that some of them may "wake up" in the next hundred years. They also believe there will be more Hawaiian Islands, but the new ones may take about 50,000 years to reach sea level.

Calliste was much younger than the Hawaiian Islands. It was probably only about one million years old. It had erupted many times, until its peak finally broke the surface of the water. With further eruptions, it continued to grow. By 1650 BCE, the round island was

The Kilauea Crater on the Big Island of Hawaii. According to legend, it is the home of Pele, the Hawaiian volcano goddess. The crater stands about 4,200 feet above sea level. Scientists believe that it began erupting at least 300,000 years ago.

about ten miles across. It had a small bay in the southern part.

It would take only a couple of hours to undo the work of a million years.

11

Mount St. Helens in Washington state erupted in 1980 and produced a massive amount of ash. It darkened the skies of the state for days. The eruption of Calliste was far greater and sent many times the amount of ash into the sky.

The Biggest Bang in History?

There are no eyewitness accounts of the eruption at Calliste, but modern scientists think they know what happened and when. They have tested different kinds of rocks and minerals on Santorini to find out their age. Their **data** points to a date close to 1650 BCE.

Scientists have also studied other eruptions to piece together what might have happened on Calliste. They have studied descriptions of the 1883 CE eruption of Krakatau, an island in modern-day Indonesia. A number of scientists believe that the explosion

A cloud of ash rises above the island of Nea Kameni in 1950. Santorini has had many smaller eruptions since the huge one in 1650 BCE.

at Calliste was far more powerful than the one at Krakatau.

The eruption of Calliste was as powerful as hundreds of atomic bombs going off at the same time. It blew a huge hole in the earth. The hole may have been as large as 30 cubic miles.

That amount of earth would cover all of New York's Manhattan Island one mile high.

The cloud from the eruption rose 20 or 30 miles into the air. The boom of the explosions could be heard hundreds of miles away. Smoke and ash would have blackened the sky for days or even weeks. It would have made a difference in the climate. Trees in California did not grow as much as normal at that time because the ash blocked the sunlight. A layer of ash in Greenland dates to about 1650 BCE. Writers in China recorded a huge cloud of ash at that time.

A large part of Calliste collapsed, making the bay much wider and deeper. The force of the explosion broke it into three smaller islands. Two on the western side were very small. The inside of the largest remaining part was a sheer cliff that dropped 800 feet straight down. Almost certainly the eruption caused a giant wave called a **tsunami** (soo-NAH-mee). It could have been several hundred feet high when it crashed ashore all around the Mediterranean. Some scientists believe that it wiped out the civilization on Crete.

A sheer cliff rises 800 feet from the harbor in Santorini. The town of Fira perches on top of the cliff.

Not everything about the eruption was destructive. Several square miles of flat land were pushed up on the eastern side of the island. The land later became very **fertile**.

Massive chunks of rock rained down all over the island. Some struck Akrotiri and

On the beach at Kamari, the "sand" is really black ash and pebbles. The huge rock that borders the beach is Mesa Vouno.

demolished many of the buildings. Soon afterward, ash began to settle. The city and the entire island were buried.

The people of Calliste may have known that the volcano would erupt. If so, they may have left in time to escape the blast. No one knows what happened to them.

An artist's idea of Atlantis. Legend says this city sank into the sea. Some people believe the legend of Atlantis began with the true story of Calliste.

Stories About Calliste

Some people believe that the eruption on Calliste appears in old stories. For example, in the Bible, God sends a series of **plagues** (PLAYGS) to the people living in Egypt. Some Bible scholars believe the plagues happened at about the time of the explosion. The eruption could explain many of the plagues, such as frogs falling from the sky.

Another old story that may be linked to Calliste is the legend of Atlantis. According to the legend, for many years Atlantis was a thriving city located on a round island. Then the people of Atlantis became wicked, and the gods decided to destroy the island. It sank into the sea and disappeared.

A horse covered in volcanic ash stands in a ruined village in Ecuador (EK-wah-dor). The ash came from the eruption of nearby Mount Tungurahua (tung-uh-RAH-wah) on August 17, 2006. The amount of deadly ash that fell after the eruption of Calliste was far greater.

Some people believe that Atlantis really existed. There are many ideas about where it was located—including on the island of Santorini.

The famous Greek thinker Plato (PLAY-toh) was the first person to describe Atlantis. Plato lived about 400 BCE. Some of his stories tell of a place similar to real descriptions of Calliste.

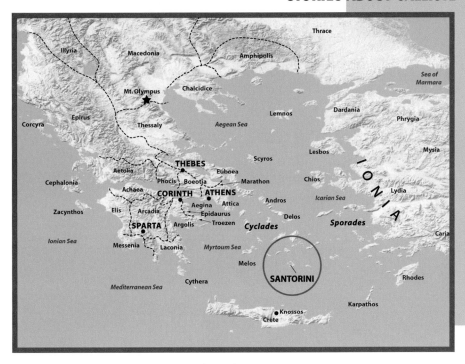

A map of Greece and Turkey (Ionia) during Plato's time shows Santorini in relation to other important Greek cities. Plato's descriptions of Atlantis may have come from altered retellings of the eruption on Calliste.

Plato wrote down stories that he said people had told him. They were about 200 to 300 years old. According to the stories, Atlantis existed 9,000 years earlier. That would have been too long ago for it to be Calliste. However, it is possible that someone made an error in writing down that number. It could have been 900 instead of 9,000, and that would make the timing of Plato's Atlantis match the timing of the eruption of Calliste.

21

Fira, the island's main town, is at the top of the 800-foot cliff on Santorini. The houses and hotels are built into the hillside.

Santorini Today

After the eruption, the island was deserted for several centuries. When people began moving back, they renamed it Thera. In the early thirteenth century CE, Venice, an important Italian city, took control of Thera. The Venetians renamed the island Santorini. The name comes from "Saint Irene."

A number of smaller, much less destructive eruptions have shaken Santorini since the one in 1650 BCE. The most recent was in 1950 CE. Their main effect was to create two small islands, Nea Kameni and Paleo Kameni, in the center of the bay.

A gently curving path with hundreds of steps connects the landing site for boats on Santorini with the town of Fira high above. Some people walk down and take the cable car back up.

Many tourists visit Santorini today. It is one of the most popular Greek islands. Fira, the island's largest town, is perched at the edge of the 800-foot cliff that was created by the eruption. People enjoy spectacular views.

Donkeys are another way to get up and down the path to Fira.

Tourists arrive at a small pier at the base of Fira's cliff, then ride a cable car to the top. Some ride donkeys along a steep zigzag path. A few hike up on foot.

In 1967, **archaeologists** (ar-kee-AH-luh-jists) began **excavating** (EX-kuh-vay-ting) the ancient city of Akrotiri. Their discoveries help us understand the city's past. The areas that

25

The island of Nea Kameni is a popular destination for Santorini visitors. Boats ferry hundreds of people to the island every day.

they have uncovered are open to tourists, who can walk along the ancient streets.

Boats also carry people to Nea Kameni. Most hike a short distance to the center of the island. There they find several small vents, which are openings in the earth. Hot steam comes out of these vents. Some people like to put their faces into this steam. While this may sound dangerous, it isn't. There isn't very much

On Nea Kameni, steam rises from vents in the earth. It shows that the island's volcano is still active.

steam. If people get uncomfortable, they only need to stand up and move a foot or two away.

Santorini is still a live volcano. Sometime another major eruption will almost certainly occur. It will probably give enough warning to allow the people who live there to escape. No one can predict how strong it will be.

TIMELINE OF MAJOR VOLCANIC ERUPTIONS

5.1 million years ago	Kauai, one of the Hawaiian Islands, begins to form
4000 BCE	A series of volcanic eruptions forms Crater Lake, Oregon
1650 BCE	Santorini Island, Greece
79 CE	Mt. Vesuvius, Italy; the eruption buries the city of Pompeii
1169	Mt. Etna, Sicily Island, Italy, causes 15,000 deaths
1631	Mt. Vesuvius, Italy
1669	Mt. Etna, Sicily Island, Italy
1783	Laki, Iceland
1815	Mt. Tambora, Indonesia (in-doe-NEE-zhuh); the following year is "the year without a summer," because ash in the atmosphere blocks sunlight for several months
1883	Krakatau, Indonesia
1902	Mount Pelée (puh-LAY), Martinique (mar-tuh-NEEK) Island, kills 30,000 people
1980	Mt. St. Helens, Washington state
1992	Mt. Pinatubo, Philippine Islands; 72 people are killed

FIND OUT MORE

Books

Arnold, Eric. *Volcanoes! Mountains of Fire.* New York: Random House Books for Young Readers, 1997.

Harris, Nicholas. *Volcano.* New York: Barron's Educational Series, 2001.

Magloff, Lisa. *Volcanoes (Eye Wonder).* New York: DK Publishing, 2003.

Roberts, Russell. *Mt. Vesuvius and the Destruction of Pompeii, A.D. 79.* Hockessin, Delaware: Mitchell Lane Publishers, 2006.

Web Sites

FEMA for Kids: Volcanoes
http://www.fema.gov/kids/volcano.htm

National Geographic Kids Magazine—Volcano: Mountain of Fire
http://www.nationalgeographic.com/ngkids/0312/

Volcanoes: Kids Research Center
http://www.gigglepotz.com/krc_volcanoes.htm

VolcanoWorld Kids' Door
http://volcano.und.edu/vwdocs/kids/kids.html

FIND OUT MORE

Works Consulted

Fisher, Richard V., Grant Heiken, and Jeffrey B. Hulen. *Volcanoes: Crucibles of Change.* Princeton, New Jersey: Princeton University Press, 1997.

Friedrich, Walter L. *Fire in the Sea.* Translated by Alexander R. McBirney. Cambridge, United Kingdom: Cambridge University Press, 2000.

Kornprobst, Jacques, and Christine Laverne. *Living Mountains: How and Why Volcanoes Erupt.* Missoula, Montana: Mountain Press Publishing Company, 2006.

History of the Island of Santorini—Thíra http://www.visit-santorini.com/site/history.htm

Lovett, Richard A. " 'Atlantis' Eruption Twice as Big as Previously Believed, Study Suggests." *National Geographic News,* August 23, 2006. http://news.nationalgeographic.com/news/2006/08/060823-thera-volcano.html

Santorini Eruption (~1630 BC) and the Legend of Atlantis http://www.geology.sdsu.edu/how_volcanoes_work/

GLOSSARY

archaeologists (ar-kee-AH-luh-jists)—People who study ancient civilizations.

civilized (SIH-vuh-lyzd)—Describes a society with an organized government, culture, and fair way of life.

data (DAA-tuh)—Factual information such as measurements or test results.

dormant (DOR-munt)—Sleeping; not currently active but capable of becoming active at a later time.

excavating (EX-kuh-vay-ting)—Digging.

fertile (FUR-tul)—Able to produce a lot of crops.

lava (LAH-vah)—Magma that has risen to Earth's surface.

magma (MAG-mah)—Molten rock under Earth's surface.

sewage (SOO-idj)—Liquid and solid waste.

tsunami (soo-NAH-mee)—A giant wave usually caused by an earthquake.

volcano (vol-KAY-noh)—A cone-shaped mountain formed by the eruption of lava, ash, and rocks.

INDEX